The Winter of 1917

A Play

David Campton

A Samuel French Acting Edition

FOUNDED 1830

SAMUELFRENCH-LONDON.CO.UK
SAMUELFRENCH.COM

Copyright © 1989 by David Campton
All Rights Reserved

THE WINTER OF 1917 is fully protected under the copyright laws of the British Commonwealth, including Canada, the United States of America, and all other countries of the Copyright Union. All rights, including professional and amateur stage productions, recitation, lecturing, public reading, motion picture, radio broadcasting, television and the rights of translation into foreign languages are strictly reserved.

ISBN 978-0-573-12299-6

www.samuelfrench-london.co.uk

www.samuelfrench.com

FOR AMATEUR PRODUCTION ENQUIRIES

UNITED KINGDOM AND WORLD EXCLUDING NORTH AMERICA

plays@SamuelFrench-London.co.uk

020 7255 4302/01

Each title is subject to availability from Samuel French,

depending upon country of performance.

CAUTION: Professional and amateur producers are hereby warned that THE WINTER OF 1917 is subject to a licensing fee. Publication of this play does not imply availability for performance. Both amateurs and professionals considering a production are strongly advised to apply to the appropriate agent before starting rehearsals, advertising, or booking a theatre. A licensing fee must be paid whether the title is presented for charity or gain and whether or not admission is charged.

The professional rights in this play are controlled by ACTAC Ltd, 15 High Street, Ramsbury, Wiltshire, SN8 2PA.

No one shall make any changes in this title for the purpose of production. No part of this book may be reproduced, stored in a retrieval system, or transmitted in any form, by any means, now known or yet to be invented, including mechanical, electronic, photocopying, recording, videotaping, or otherwise, without the prior written permission of the publisher. No one shall upload this title, or part of this title, to any social media websites.

The right of David Campton to be identified as author of this work has been asserted by him in accordance with Section 77 of the Copyright, Designs and Patents Act 1988

CHARACTERS

Truepenny. Pleasant and intelligent—takes charge almost unconsciously

Bascomb. Rough and rebellious: questions everything—especially orders

Clegg. Cheerful and willing, though not over-bright

Wynn. Self-centred: when things go wrong, will always find someone else to blame

Higgs One. Agreeable—always agrees with the last speaker

Higgs Two. Higgs One's twin—though not necessarily identical

The action takes place in a ground floor room of a large country house

---

If this play is produced with a mixed cast, Truepenny should be male and Clegg female. Otherwise casting depends on the availability of performers

PRODUCTION NOTES

The door should be hinged downstage. This way a stage manager can open, shut or hold the door without being seen by the audience.

The knocking on the door should be done either on the stage floor or on a separate piece of wood. (It is impossible to beat on the actual door without shaking the set.)

The lights and firelight can either be brought up gradually from the onset of the off-stage voices or suddenly as the door opens: but they must be synchronised—do not bring one up without the other.

The furniture can be as lavish or as spare as the designer wishes, but the characters should not use it (certainly not sit on any of the chairs). Although apparently solid they exist in fact in a different time. Just as, apart from Truepenny, no one can feel the fire.

D.C.

THE WINTER OF 1917

A downstairs room in a large country house. At CURTAIN *rise it is in complete darkness*

Offstage a pane of glass is broken. After a slight pause there is a shuffling and the sound of voices as a group makes its way through the house

Truepenny (*off*) Did you have to break that window?
Bascomb (*off*) We had to get in.
Clegg (*off*) Is this somebody's house?
Bascomb (*off*) All houses are somebody's house.
Wynn (*off*) Doesn't that make us burglars?
Bascomb (*off*) Back out if you like.
Higgs One (*off*) But we're all soaking.
Higgs Two (*off*) Soaking.
Bascomb (*off*) Who's got the torch?
Higgs One (*off*) Torch, anybody?
Clegg (*off*) I've got a box of matches.
Bascomb (*off*) Then let's be having a light.
Truepenny (*off*) There must be a door somewhere.
Higgs One (*off*) Where?
Higgs Two (*off*) Ouch!
Bascomb (*off*) Where's that light?
Clegg (*off*) I've dropped the matches.
Wynn (*off*) Trust you!
Clegg (*off*) If somebody shone the torch, I could look for them.
Bascomb (*off*) If somebody could find the torch, you wouldn't *need* to look for 'em.
Clegg (*off*) They were wet anyway.
Truepenny (*off*) I said there was a door. Here.

As the door is opened, the room is flooded with light. It is comfortably furnished with a fire in the grate. It looks as though its well-to-do owners had just stepped out for a minute

A group is crowded in the doorway. They are bedraggled, but dressed for dealing with adverse conditions

There is a slight pause as they take in their surroundings

Clegg It's a room!
Bascomb What else did you expect to find behind a door?
Wynn Where did the light come from?
Bascomb Where does light usually come from?
Higgs One And look at that fire.
Higgs Two Warmth.
Clegg An' dryth. (*He makes for it*)
Wynn Hold on.
Clegg (*standing in front of it*) Lovely.
Wynn Bash said the place was empty.
Bascomb Who said they couldn't walk another step?
Wynn What's going to happen when somebody finds us dripping all over their carpet?
Truepenny If the worst comes to the worst, they can throw us out.
Clegg They wouldn't, would they? I mean, we've only just got here.
Bascomb If the worst comes to the worst, they can dial 999.
Wynn You're the one who broke the window.
Bascomb You were quick enough to follow.
Truepenny (*looking around*) I have a feeling about this place.
Wynn You and your feelings. If it weren't for them we shouldn't be here at all.
Clegg (*cheerfully*) That's right. We'd still be lost in the woods.
Higgs One Without a compass.
Bascomb (*angrily*) Oh, shut up!
Higgs Two (*to Higgs One*) What did you say?
Wynn These folk have got to be well-off. Not the sort who offer burglars cups of tea.
Truepenny (*thoughtfully*) Just who are—they?
Wynn They've got to be the Upstairs sort.
Higgs One Upstairs?
Wynn Like we're all Downstairs sort.
Bascomb They might even be the Jeeves-pass-the-horsewhip sort; the keep-the-peasants-in-their-place sort.
Truepenny (*indicating the dark beyond the door*) I mean—look out there—in the hall. Bare boards. Nothing but enormous stairs going up to nowhere. What sort of people live nowhere?
Bascomb I can't be bothered with riddles. (*He strides to the fire*)

The Winter of 1917

You lot, when you've finished steaming, let somebody else feel the fire. (*He elbows the others out of the way*)
Truepenny I could—look for them.
Clegg You mean—explain what we're doing here?
Truepenny If you like.
Wynn And the broken window?
Truepenny That is—if . . .
Bascomb Backing out already?
Higgs Two If what?
Truepenny Oh, I'm sure they'll listen to reason. Most people do if you talk reasonably.
Clegg There must be a lot of rooms. Would you like one of us to come, too?
Wynn Don't ask me.
Truepenny Actually, I wasn't going to ask anyone.
Wynn Creeping round an old ruin in the middle of the night. A person could get lost—if not worse.
Truepenny There are no secret passages, no dungeons.
Wynn How do you know?
Truepenny It's just an ordinary house. Big—not haunted.
Bascomb Want a bet?
Clegg Shall I come with you?
Truepenny There's really no need. (*He picks up a matchbox near the door*) Here are your matches, Clegg.
Clegg Take them. Will there be enough to light you while you're out there?
Truepenny I expect I'll see all I'm meant to see.
Bascomb What's that supposed to mean?
Truepenny I'll let you know when I get back.

Truepenny exits

Bascomb Don't be such a tassel! (*He goes to the door and shouts after Truepenny*) It's about time you dropped this True-Blue-Harold act. Whatever we're in for could be bad enough without going to meet it half-way.
Higgs One What do you mean—in for?
Higgs Two What do you mean—bad enough?
Bascomb Expect the worst and you won't be disappointed.
Clegg Oh, that's all right then.
Wynn All right?

Clegg Well, the worst I can think of right now is being turned out into the rain again, and I know what that's like, so the worst may not be so bad after all.
Bascomb I'm surrounded by flopears!
Clegg What do you suppose Truepenny's going to find?
Bascomb Francis Adams. But that doesn't matter if there's a Brownie point to be picked up. Truepenny's asking for another gold star at the end of this stinking initiative test. Initiative test! What are we doing here anyway?
Clegg Testing our initiative.
Bascomb We are here because the silly schlurp running the show came up with a spiffing idea. "Hey, you chaps, how about dumping 'em in the middle of nowhere? Better—let's pick a day when the weathermen forecast wind, rain, snow, sleet, thunder, lightning and hell-fire."
Clegg I don't remember hell-fire in the forecast.
Bascomb "Better still, let's lumber 'em with Truepenny. If they can put up with Truepenny, they can put up with anything. Because Truepenny is one of your 'Follow-me-chaps' types."
Clegg They said this course was to encourage leadership. They said we are all potential leaders.
Bascomb Dying to be a leader, Clegg?
Clegg I've never thought much about it.
Bascomb You lot . . .
Higgs One Who?
Bascomb You're born followers.
Higgs Two Are we?
Bascomb You troop after Truepenny like so many bleating sheep. Don't you ever think for yourselves?
Wynn You're the one who suggested the short cut through the woods.
Higgs One Without a compass.
Bascomb Are you trying to start an argument?
Clegg I was told this course helps you to find yourself.
Bascomb Were you lost?
Wynn Not 'till we took the short cut.
Bascomb If we hadn't taken that short cut, we'd still be out soaking in the fields.
Clegg True enough. If we hadn't taken the short cut, we'd never have found this place.

Bascomb I can't feel the fire. Will one of you fancies shut the door?

Clegg If we shut the door, the light won't shine out for Truepenny.

Bascomb Too bad. (*He strides to the door and kicks it shut*)

Clegg But Bash ...

Bascomb The name's Bascomb.

Clegg I thought you liked to be called Bash.

Bascomb Since when did you give a tinker's for what I like?

Clegg Anyway Truepenny's got some matches now. ... As long as they hold out. ... As long as they're not too wet. As long as ...

Bascomb As long as what?

Clegg Don't know yet. I'm trying to think of something cheerful to say.

Bascomb Don't strain yourself.

Clegg (*with rather desperate cheerfulness*) This is a nice place.

Higgs Two Nice.

Wynn It gives me the shivers.

Clegg It looks so—lived in.

Wynn That's what gives me the shivers. Suppose ...

Higgs One Suppose what?

Bascomb Stop supposing, will you? It's here. We're here. That's all we know. That's all we need to know.

Clegg As though they'd only stepped out for a minute.

Wynn Who?

Clegg Whoever they were.

Wynn Why did you say "were"?

Clegg When they were here they were, weren't they?

Wynn I mean, why not say "are"?

Clegg Well, they're not here now, are they?

Bascomb A half-witted parrot could talk better sense.

Clegg I mean—well—look here ... (*He examines articles left lying on the table without actually touching them*) Gloves—white.

Higgs One Gloves.

Clegg Glass—empty.

Higgs Two Empty glass.

Clegg Cigar—half-smoked—and this looks like a sort of programme. "One step. Veleta. Waltz. Schottische. Tango." Aren't they dances?

Bascomb They're not fizzy drinks.

Wynn This is all so creepy.
Clegg What's creepy about dances?
Wynn They're old. There's nothing in this room that wasn't old when Granny was a girl. Why should anybody want to keep a place looking like this?
Clegg Perhaps they're old as well.
Wynn Like a museum.
Bascomb If only this clotty place could have turned out to be a comfortable ruin. With just enough roof left on to keep out the weather. That's what I was prepared for.
Clegg This is better, isn't it?
Bascomb This is a mystery.
Higgs Two Mystery?
Bascomb I don't like mysteries. ... And I still can't feel that flaming fire.
Clegg It's flaming all right. I can see the flames.
Bascomb Can you feel 'em?
Clegg I wouldn't expect to.
Higgs One Not from over here.
Bascomb Even when you were over there, buggins. Did you feel anything?
Clegg I didn't think about it. I was glad to be in front of a fire.
Bascomb The back of your jeans was half-way up the chimney.
Wynn These big houses always are freezing.
Higgs Two Always.
Bascomb Try warming your hands.
Wynn Why?
Bascomb You're nearest the fireplace.
Wynn (*edging away from it*) You're the one complaining. Why don't you go back to it?
Bascomb There's something fantastic about that fire. As though— as though ...
Clegg Go on.
Bascomb As though it wasn't really there.
Wynn We can believe our eyes, can't we?
Bascomb What about the rest of you? I bet you could put your hand in that fire and not feel a thing.
Wynn You be me.
Bascomb If you want a thing doing ... (*He crosses to the fireplace*)
Clegg You're never going to ...

Wynn Don't be so wet.
Bascomb Me? Wet? (*He kneels by the fireplace*) Watch my hand, Wynn. Nearer and nearer.
Wynn Are you trying to make me feel sick?
Bascomb I'm trying to make you believe me.
Clegg I'll believe you if you want me to.
Bascomb You don't count. You'd believe anything.
Clegg I mean you don't have to do anything daft just to convince us.
Bascomb Perhaps I want to convince myself. (*He takes a deep breath and holds his hand out over the flames*) There.
Wynn (*turning away*) Tell me when it's all over.
Bascomb (*wonderingly, his hand still over the fire*) There. There.
Higgs One Oh!
Wynn Who's got the first aid kit?
Clegg Doesn't that hurt?
Bascomb What's it look like?
Wynn I'm not looking.
Bascomb What sort of fire would you call that?
Wynn What do you do for an encore—the rope trick?
Bascomb Maybe. (*He stands up*) Right now I'm wondering what sort of place we've got ourselves into.
Wynn I don't know and I don't care. Rain or not, I've had enough of it.
Clegg We can't leave without Truepenny.
Higgs Two No.
Bascomb (*sarcastically*) Can't do a thing without follow-my-leader Truepenny.
Higgs One What *are* we going to do?
Bascomb Think.
Higgs Two Think?
Bascomb Those of us who *can* think. Those who can't—shut up.
Clegg Sorry.
Bascomb We've all seen phoney fires before. Electric flickers. Like the real thing but nobody has to keep running to the coal-place. Nothing to bring anybody out in a sweat.
Wynn Who's in a sweat?
Bascomb That's all right then. We'll sit back and wait for old Truepenny.
Clegg If you say so, Bash.

Bascomb What? Oh, no you don't.
Clegg Don't what?
Bascomb Whatever you do you'll do because *you* want to do it. Understood?
Wynn If that's what you want.
Bascomb Want? I don't want a doddling thing. If you want somebody to play follow-my-leader with, don't count on me. Nobody ought to tell anybody what to do. Nobody ought to be expected to tell anybody what to do. I've had a belly-full of that bull already.
Wynn What brought that on?
Bascomb Tell us what to do so we'll know who to blame when anything goes wrong. Bash said "Let's take the short cut", so we wouldn't be here at all if it wasn't for Bash. Bash broke the window to let us in, so whatever happens now is Bash's fault.
Clegg Nobody said that, Bash.
Bascomb Let 'em all be leaders who want.
Clegg I never heard anybody say it.
Bascomb Bash ain't taking that on.
Clegg Did you hear anybody say it?
Bascomb Leave all that mush to Truepenny.
Wynn Truepenny's a long time coming back.
Bascomb That's up to Truepenny.
Wynn What if ...
Bascomb What if what?
Wynn Doesn't matter.

Short pause

Clegg Hark.
Wynn Huh?
Clegg The rain's stopped.
Higgs One Has it?
Higgs Two Yes.
Bascomb Good.
Clegg I can't hear it against the window.
Bascomb You won't if it's stopped.
Clegg I suppose not.
Wynn If the rain's stopped, we can ...
Higgs One Yes.
Clegg As soon as ...

Wynn What's Truepenny playing at?
Higgs Two Ah.
Wynn Don't give a fiddle for us hanging about. Biting our nails. Wondering.
Bascomb That's one of your leader's perks. Other ranks aren't supposed to wonder. Theirs but to do or die.
Wynn But what if Truepenny ...
Bascomb Did? Or died?
Wynn Truepenny's only looking for the—the others.
Bascomb Oh, yes?
Clegg What do you suppose Truepenny found?
Wynn Don't talk daft.
Clegg I only asked.
Bascomb Suppose—only suppose, mind—Truepenny don't ... How long before we—?
Wynn Clear out?
Bascomb Not what I was going to suggest. But reasonable. Very reasonable. I certainly wouldn't ask anybody else to take a risk on that stupid bonzo's account.
Clegg Do you think ... ?
Bascomb I stopped thinking back in the woods.
Wynn What—could be out there—in the other rooms?
Bascomb You've got a choice. Either wait to be put in the picture or go and find out for yourself. I reckon ...
Higgs One What?
Bascomb This place is getting even colder.
Clegg Pity about the fire.
Bascomb Pity I shut that door.
Clegg You had to keep the draught out.
Bascomb Now I've got to open it again. Take more of an effort. Especially when you're not sure what's on the other side. ... So ... If you hear me shout ...
Clegg We'll come running.
Bascomb Don't be nutters. Get out of here fast. (*He crosses to the door*)

At the same time it opens and Truepenny comes in

Bascomb is halted and Wynn gives an involuntary squeal

Don't you reckon to knock?
Clegg What did you find out there?

Truepenny Nothing.
Higgs Two Nothing?
Truepenny No vampires, werewolves or mad axemen.
Higgs One Oh.
Bascomb Disappointed?
Truepenny This ruin really is some place. Wild life moved in upstairs: I could hear them tweeting and scuffling. There's one room on the other side of the house big enough to hold a ball in. The moon's full on the windows. Fantastic.
Clegg What about people? What did they say?
Truepenny I told you—there are no people. Mice, yes. Owls maybe. But the people must have moved out ages ago.
Bascomb Leaving one room like this?
Truepenny There must be an explanation. I've no idea what. I suggest we make the most of what we've got while we've got it.
Bascomb If the storm's over, there's nothing to keep us here.
Truepenny Only this touch of comfort. Remember you've been enjoying it while I was exploring. (*He crouches by the fire*)
Wynn I wouldn't say "enjoying". Bash—didn't you say we ought to be on our way.
Bascomb I said do whatever you want. Don't look to me for orders.
Truepenny We'll move on in a while, Wynn. Just give me a chance to warm through first. The chill out there could strike through any thermal underwear.
Clegg You won't get much joy out of that fire.
Truepenny Why not?
Higgs One We've tried.
Truepenny But it's gorgeous.
Bascomb Gorgeous is as gorgeous does.
Truepenny (*warming his hands*) That's better. My fingers were frozen.
Clegg You mean you can really feel some heat?
Truepenny Why shouldn't I? Glowing red coals. Just right for toast.

Truepenny stands and turns. Wynn looks from Truepenny to Bascomb and back again. Slight pause

Clegg You wouldn't like to put *your* hand in the fire, would you?

Truepenny Put my ...?
Clegg The way Bash did.

Pause

Truepenny I seem to have missed a couple of chapters.
Higgs One That fire's a fake.
Truepenny Not on the back of *my* legs.
Bascomb You believe what you want to believe: I'll believe what I want to believe.
Truepenny What *do* you believe?
Bascomb There's something going on that I don't understand, and the sooner I'm out of it, the better.
Truepenny There's something I don't understand either—and the sooner I get to the bottom of it, the better.
Wynn Does that matter now?
Truepenny To me it does.
Bascomb Please yourself.
Truepenny So ... (*He considers the things on the table*) What do you make of these?
Wynn Do we have to make anything?
Truepenny He took the gloves off because he didn't want tobacco stains on them. White gloves, you see. So it must have been a fairly formal affair, even out here in the wilds.
Wynn Are we expected to stick around while you play Sherlock Holmes?
Truepenny Men used to wear gloves at a dance. No sweaty hands on ladies' dresses.
Bascomb I suppose you'll tell us next what they've been drinking.
Truepenny Champagne.
Clegg How do you know that?
Bascomb Shape of the glass.
Wynn Then where are "They"?
Truepenny (*vaguely*) Out there—somewhere—I suppose.
Higgs Two Out there?
Clegg But you spent ages searching. Nothing but mice and moonlight you said.
Wynn All this gets madder by the minute.
Bascomb You mean Truepenny does.
Truepenny As though he put the cigar down only a little while ago.

Bascomb It's a flaming mirage.

Clegg Like you get in the desert?

Bascomb (*looking out through the open door*) There's nothing in this house but damp walls and cobwebs. So why should we be seeing ... ?

Clegg Besides, we're not in the desert.

Wynn I've had enough. You lot ready to make tracks?

Higgs One I am.

Higgs Two Me, too.

Bascomb But not Truepenny. Not old stiff-upper-lip-an'-play-the-game Truepenny. Never show the other ranks you're scared, eh?

Truepenny Who's scared?

Bascomb I am and I don't care who knows it.

Truepenny Animals are afraid of things they don't understand. People try to find out what's going on. We're people.

Bascomb So what's going on?

Truepenny There must have been a ball here.

Higgs Two Here?

Truepenny In that moonlit room, I suppose.

Bascomb Now. What's happening now?

Truepenny This card hasn't been marked. She wasn't expecting to dance.

Wynn Does that matter now?

Truepenny I see her as a very confused lady.

Bascomb You stop seeing things and come down to the level of us trogs.

Truepenny They must have been very confusing times—the winter of nineteen seventeen.

Higgs One Nineteen seventeen?

Truepenny The war should have been over in six months, but it was dragging on and on.

Higgs Two What war?

Clegg How do you know so much about it?

Truepenny Doesn't everybody?

Higgs One I don't.

Truepenny I feel as though I'd always known. As though I was ...

Bascomb There?

Truepenny (*half listening to something outside*) "The Merry Widow" for the sobersides—"Alexander's Ragtime Band" for the moderns.

The Winter of 1917

Bascomb Were you going to say "There"?
Truepenny Nothing *too* modern, though. After all, nobody wants to be reminded that this is the winter of nineteen seventeen. No khaki among the dancers. Even those on leave want to forget the colour of mud. Especially those on leave.
Bascomb Listen to me, Truepenny.
Truepenny Champagne at midnight. Fruit punch before. Wartime economy.
Bascomb To me. (*He kicks the door shut*) There is no dance going on.
Truepenny Then why can I hear . . . ?
Bascomb You can't.
Truepenny This room was waiting.
Wynn I said we shouldn't have broken in.
Truepenny In the winter of nineteen seventeen. For them.
Bascomb But they're not here. We are.
Truepenny Any moment now that door will open, and they'll come in.
Wynn You don't mean—like ghosts?
Clegg Don't be daft. Nobody believes in ghosts.
Truepenny They're as real as these gloves and cigar.
Wynn If they were alive in nineteen seventeen, they could be dead now.
Truepenny They'll always be alive in nineteen seventeen.
Bascomb What does that mean?
Clegg But we're not in nineteen seventeen. We're now.
Truepenny Are you so sure?
Clegg I'm alive. I'd know if I wasn't, wouldn't I?
Truepenny They're more alive than you'll ever be.
Clegg I'm not sure that was a nice thing to say.
Wynn There's nobody here but us.
Higgs Two Us.
Wynn You said so.
Truepenny What did I say?
Wynn You said this place was empty.
Higgs Two Empty.
Truepenny Why did I say that?
Clegg You searched.
Truepenny The dancers waltz on, but a couple have slipped away. Things need to be said. In here.

The door opens. All watch fascinated. No one comes in but Truepenny seems to see them

Bascomb Strong wind.
Truepenny He's holding the door open for her.
Clegg Who's holding the what for who?
Truepenny (*watching*) In his hands are a pair of gloves. She's holding an empty glass. They're putting them on the table.
Wynn You're making this up.
Bascomb Like I said—so much wind.

Bascomb crosses to the door, but it swings shut of its own accord before it can be reached. Bascomb is left speechless

Clegg Can the wind suck as well as blow?
Truepenny *He* shut the door.
Wynn There is no "he". Not here.
Truepenny He crosses to the fire.
Clegg You're kidding us, aren't you?
Truepenny She stands turning a ring on her finger. Third finger, left hand. A diamond catches the light.
Clegg You can't really see anything, can you, True?
Truepenny She speaks. "What did you say to Father?" she asks. "He turned quite pale, then very pink."
Bascomb Word for word, is it?
Truepenny "Was it bad news? Has your leave been cancelled? Don't say you have to go back before the wedding."
Clegg This isn't funny any longer. I'm not going to laugh.
Truepenny He says, "I told him I shall not be going back." She says, "Have you been promoted to the War Office?"
Wynn That's not what we want to know.
Higgs One No.
Higgs Two Definitely not.
Truepenny Silence becomes unbearable and she rattles on ... (*He looks at each imaginary speaker in turn*) "Father says there's nothing wrong with the war effort that better leadership wouldn't put right. He says the men are just waiting to be led to victory. He believes you're a born officer." He says, "He's wrong."
Higgs One Oh.
Wynn What's got into Truepenny?

The Winter of 1917

Bascomb I don't know. But I bet it isn't doing any good there.
Truepenny She says, "Don't be so modest, darling. You're our local hero—with a Military Cross to prove it. He says, "What does a medal prove?"
Wynn That doesn't sound like Truepenny talking.
Bascomb It isn't Truepenny. Truepenny doesn't even think like that.
Truepenny He says, "Over there is another world. If we don't talk about it much, that's because we can't find the words. I want you to understand ..." She says, "What is there to understand?"
Clegg Truepenny?
Truepenny He says, "Over there a sort of madness sets in, then there's no telling the difference between battle-field and playing field".
Clegg You're with us, not with them—whoever they are.
Truepenny "Mills bombs for cricket balls, that's all".
Bascomb You're not getting through, Cleggers.
Truepenny "Only when you lead a team out on to that pitch, most of them don't live to learn the score."
Clegg Let's go now, True.
Truepenny She says, "We were told you carried one of the wounded to safety on your shoulder, under enemy fire".
Clegg Please.
Truepenny He says, "One of twenty. The others lay where they fell. Men—not runs or goals or points. Men."
Wynn Do we have to stay and listen to that stuff?
Bascomb I'm not telling you to.
Wynn Right. (*He goes to the door and tries to open it, but cannot*)
Truepenny "Over here, looking back, I'm able to grasp what a monstrous perversion it is of all we were ever taught. But I know too, that once I'm over there again the madness will return. Play up! Play up! Play the game! Leading men to their graves isn't a game: it's an obscenity. That's why I can't go back."
Clegg I don't want to hear any more.
Truepenny I'm sorry, my dear. We may never have the chance to talk together again.
Wynn The door. It won't open.
Higgs One Won't.–?
Bascomb Don't be daft.

Wynn You try then.

Bascomb tries to open the door with no better success

Truepenny Not after you return my ring and your father forbids me the house.
Wynn Well?
Bascomb Hell!
Wynn Locked?
Higgs One It can't be.
Clegg You really mean it!
Truepenny I mean it.
Clegg If you refuse, what will happen to you?
Truepenny A Court Martial—unless some officious medico diagnoses insanity and has me put away. But I have not lost my senses. I believe I've come to them.
Clegg I'm afraid for you. Aren't you afraid?
Truepenny Only of being thought afraid. My weakest point. Will you try to take advantage of it?
Wynn Why?
Bascomb Why ask me?
Truepenny I can tell you now that not even cries of "coward" will drive me back to that. I will no longer be responsible for other men's lives—or their deaths. Especially not their deaths.
Clegg Someone has to be.
Bascomb Not you, too, Clegg.
Truepenny Not me.
Clegg With a good officer leading, will they be more or less likely to die?
Truepenny Now you're talking like your father.
Higgs One Not like Clegg.
Higgs Two That's for sure.
Bascomb I don't want to hear any more.
Higgs One Nor me.
Wynn Do something.
Bascomb Why don't you?
Wynn What can we do?
Bascomb That's up to you. Do whatever you like.
Wynn (*shouting*) But we don't know what to do.
Bascomb (*shouting back*) So why should I know?
Clegg Will anything I say make a scrap of difference?

Truepenny How can any officer lead unless he believes in what he is doing?
Clegg Are you against the war now?
Truepenny No, no, no. Only against leaders.
Clegg Theirs or ours?
Truepenny All. All. All.
Higgs Two What is the matter with them?
Truepenny Every one who led us into this morass.
Bascomb I'd say they were stuck in the middle of last week.
Higgs One Last week?
Bascomb Or the middle of nineteen seventeen.
Higgs One Stuck?
Higgs Two Them?
Bascomb Or whatever got into them.
Wynn Suppose it gets to us. We're trapped in here. With— whatever it is ... Open this door.
Bascomb How?
Higgs One Tell us what to do.
Higgs Two Somebody.
Wynn Anybody.
Bascomb Oh, pull yourselves together.
Truepenny All those born leaders with all those corpses on their consciences. If conscience wasn't the first casualty. What price a thousand mangled bodies if there's a yard of mud to be gained? Are you asking me to rejoin the death or glory boys, shouting "follow me, men" ...? I'll put a bullet through my own brain first.
Clegg This is madness!

There is a knock at the door. Truepenny and Clegg glance towards it, then stand unmoving, with bated breath

Wynn The door.
Higgs One Open it.
Higgs Two I can't. It won't.
Bascomb Listen, you lot. We've got to get through to them somehow.
Wynn We can't.
Bascomb We can try.
Wynn Let us out.
Higgs One Out.

Higgs Two Out.
Bascomb Listen! We've got to bring 'em back to here and now.
Wynn We've got to get away.
Higgs Two Help!
Higgs Two Help!
Bascomb Because I can't see us getting anywhere until we do.
Wynn There's nothing we can do.
Bascomb There's nobody else to do it.

The knock is repeated

Clegg It's Father.
Truepenny I know.
Wynn Let us out.
Higgs One Open up.
Higgs Two Open.
Bascomb I reckon that door won't open 'till one of them opens it.
Higgs One Who?
Higgs Two Which one?
Wynn Who cares? Help us.
Clegg He's expecting an answer.
Truepenny Such as "Sorry, sir. Just a touch of shell shock"?
Clegg Perhaps it is.
Higgs One ⎫
Higgs Two ⎭ (*together*) Help!
Bascomb For Santa's sake stop flapping like headless chickens.
Truepenny I am not confused. I can see clearly—perhaps for the first time in my life. If you open that door to him, there'll be no time left for us ...
Clegg We were so proud of you.
Truepenny You may still have reason to be.

Another knock. Wynn and the Twins fall to their knees, wailing

Bascomb That's not going to help.
Truepenny If my life could shorten this war by one day, I'd give it gladly. But I'll not lead any more men like so many sheep to the butcher.
Bascomb On your feet, there. Look lively.

Another knock

Clegg He won't go away.

Truepenny Can their ghosts be laid by spilling more blood? And *that* spilled blood by spilling more? Will nothing less than a bloody Niagara suffice? Somebody must cry Stop!
Clegg This is me you're talking to. *Me*!
Truepenny Are you with me or for him?
Clegg I don't know. I don't know.
Bascomb Are you jerks going to snivel all night?
Truepenny Are you so afraid of him?

Another knock

Bascomb Jump to it.
Higgs One
Higgs Two (*together*) Us?
Bascomb Am I talking to myself?
Truepenny Are you?
Clegg (*unconvinced*) No.
Truepenny Then tell him so.

Another knock

Bascomb Listen to me. Listen.
Truepenny Tell him. For my sake—tell him.
Bascomb Tell him to flake off.
Clegg I—can't.

Another knock

Bascomb Tell him to get lost ... Hear me? Get lost. Get—lost. ... Join in, you jellybabies. Follow my lead.
Higgs One Follow you?
Truepenny Will you stand by me?
Bascomb If you can't do anything else you can shout. So shout. Get lost.
Higgs Two Are you telling us?
Bascomb I'm telling you. Shout.
Truepenny Without you I don't think I can go on.
Bascomb Oh, no you don't. There's no cosy way out for you either. Shout "get lost" with the rest of us. Everybody after me. Get lost. Get knotted. Hop it. Scarper.

Continuous knocking

Go away.

Higgs One Go away?
Bascomb Louder. Go away.

Wynn and the Twins start a continuous chant of "go away" against the knocking

Truepenny I've faced death often enough, but I think I've never been nearer than now.
Bascomb That's just bellyaching.
Clegg He only thinks what everybody else will be saying.
Truepenny Then disown me or disown them.
Bascomb Stand up for yourself. . . . Don't stop, you lot. Go away. Go away.
Clegg Go—away.
Bascomb That's right. After me. Go away.
Clegg Go away.
Truepenny What?
Bascomb Yes, you as well. Shout "go away."
Truepenny Go—away?
Bascomb All together. Go away.
All Go away. Go away. Go away.
Bascomb Out out out.
All Out. Out out.
Bascomb Go. Go. Go.
All Go. Go. Go.

The knocking stops

Clegg suddenly stumbles, clutching his head. The door flies open. Truepenny reels, hand to head. The door is slammed shut. Slight pause. Bascomb crosses to the door. It opens easily

Bascomb Hello, out there? . . . Nothing. See? Still nothing.
Truepenny (*dazed*) Where—where are they?
Wynn Gone.
Higgs One Whover they were.
Higgs Two Whatever they were.
Truepenny But—gone?
Wynn Bash did it.
Clegg Did what?
Bascomb Nothing.
Truepenny The door opened—and they . . . And . . . But now . . .

The Winter of 1917

Clegg Something happened in between. What?
Truepenny I'm trying to remember.
Bascomb Don't try too hard.
Truepenny (*hand to head*) I feel ...
Clegg So do I.
Truepenny Odd.
Wynn What now?
Bascomb What do you mean—what now?
Wynn Back to the woods?
Bascomb Are you still asking me?
Clegg Why not stay here?
Wynn If that's a joke, I'm not laughing.
Clegg After all, there's a fire.
Higgs One Oh no, there's not.
Higgs Two It's gone out.

They all look at the grate, which is now dark. The Lights too are dimmer

Bascomb We'd better be going, too. And fast.
Wynn Do you know the way?
Bascomb All right. Follow me. Come on.
Truepenny But ...
Bascomb I said "Come on". Get your packs out of here and be quick about it. (*He makes shooing movements*)

The Twins hurry out

Wynn Nobody can change history, can they?
Bascomb What's history? Move before you get caught up in it again.

Wynn hurries out

Clegg I wonder—what *did* happen here in nineteen seventeen?

Clegg goes out

Bascomb Does that matter now?
Truepenny Only to them. And they're all gone anyway. Aren't they? I wonder ...
Bascomb You as well?
Truepenny Will this room still be here—like this—after we've gone?

Bascomb We'll never know, shall we? Because we shan't be here. Now come on.

Bascomb goes out

Truepenny If you say so.

Truepenny goes out

After a slight pause the door swings shut and the Lights fade

CURTAIN

FURNITURE AND PROPERTY LIST

On stage: Table. *On it*: man's white gloves, empty champagne glass, dance card
Chairs
Fire grate. *In it:* fire
Mantelpiece
Matchbox near door
Other dressing as desired

LIGHTING PLOT

One interior set. Fittings required: fire

To open: Darkness

Cue 1	As door opens *Flood room with light. Fire alight in grate*	(Page 1)
Cue 2	After door flies open *Gradually dim lights and fire glow*	(Page 20)
Cue 3	Door swings shut *Fade to black-out*	(Page 22)

EFFECTS PLOT

Cue 1   Before C<small>URTAIN</small> rises   (Page 1)
Rain effect. Continue until page 8

Cue 2   As C<small>URTAIN</small> rises   (Page 1)
Glass breaking

www.ingramcontent.com/pod-product-compliance
Lightning Source LLC
Chambersburg PA
CBHW070456050426
42450CB00012B/3298